TONGUES-SPEAKING

TONGUES-SPEAKING
The Meaning, Purpose, and Cessation of Tongues

Kenneth L. Gentry, Jr., Th.D.

VICTORIOUS HOPE
P.U.B.L.I.S.H.I.N.G

Fountain Inn, South Carolina 29644

"Proclaiming the kingdom of God and teaching those things
which concern the Lord Jesus Christ, with all confidence."
(Acts 28:31)

Tongues-Speaking:
The Meaning, Purpose, and Cessation of Tongues

Fourth edition Copyright © 2014 by Gentry Family Trust udt April 2, 1999.

Published by Victorious Hope Publishing
P.O. Box 1874
Fountain Inn, South Carolina 29644

Website: www.VictoriousHope.com

Kenneth Gentry websites:
— Commercial website: www.KennethGentry.com
— Research ministry website: www.GoodBirthMinistries.com
— Blog site: www.PostmillennialismToday.com

Printed in the United States of America

ISBN: 978-0-9826206-7-0

Cover design by Kevin Slack.

VICTORIOUS HOPE PUBLISHING is committed to producing Christian educational materials for promoting the whole Bible for the whole of life. We are conservative, evangelical, and Reformed and are committed to the doctrinal formulation found in the Westminster Standards.

TABLE OF CONTENTS

ANALYTICAL OUTLINE

I. Introduction

II. The Form of Tongues: Communication
    A. Tongues Were Structured Languages
        1. Argument from First Occurrence
        2. Argument from Later Episodes
        3. Argument from Identical Terminology
        4. Argument from Language Analogy
        5. Argument from Biblical Principle
    B. Alleged Negative Passages
        1. First Corinthians 14:2
        2. First Corinthians 14:14
        3. First Corinthians 13:1
        4. Romans 8:26

III. The Content of Tongues: Revelation
    A. Argument from Initial Occurrence
    B. Argument from Word-gift Relationship
    C. Argument from Mystery Character
    D. Conclusion

IV. The Purpose of Tongues: Confirmation
    A. Miracles as Validation in the Old Testament
    B. Miracles as Validation in the New Covenant

V. The Purpose of Tongues: Admonition
    A. Covenantal Backdrop
    B. Covenantal Sign
    C. Covenantal Tongues
    D. Covenantal Judgment
    E. Covenantal Unbelief
        1. The Corinthian Context

Chapter 1
INTRODUCTION

Knowledgeable Christians are aware that a long-standing charismatic revival is all about us. The charismatic movement is so vigorous that it has become one of the most phenomenal religious movements of our time. Its presence is dramatically felt in America and throughout the world. A 2011 Pew Foundation study discovered that there are 305 million charismatic Christians and 279 million Pentecostals in the world.[1]

The movement is also multi-faceted, boasting a wide variety of charismatic experiences among its adherents. These experiences include prophetic utterances, miraculous healings, being "slain in the Spirit," "holy laughter,"and so forth. Nevertheless, speaking in tongues (or *glossolalia*, as it is technically known) is certainly one of the most distinctive features of the movement.

In this book I will briefly investigate the Scriptural data regarding four fundamental issues relating to tongues-speaking. After a basic introduction to the matter (chapter 1), I will answer four key questions:

1. What was the structural form of tongues?
    In chapter 2 I will answer whether they were formal languages or unstructured emotional praises. This is an important initial question for analyzing the modern tongues movement.

---

[1] See: "Global Christianity – A Report on the Size and Distribution of the World's Christian Population" from the Pew Foundation: http://www.pewforum.org/2011/12/19/global-christianity-exec/ "Charismatic" Christians are closely related to Pentecostals, except that they are generally found in main-stream churches rather than historically recognized Pentecostalist churches.

2. What was the specific content of tongues?
    In chapter 3 I will focus on whether they brought author-
    itative revelation of God's will or were simply opportunities
    of personal praise and uplift. This is a question with signif-
    icant implications for the role of tongues in the church and
    the Christian life.

3. What was the purpose of tongues?
    In chapters 4 and 5, I will consider their two fundamental
    purposes relative to the apostles as well as to redemptive-
    history. There we will learn their significance for the apos-
    tles themselves, as well as their place in redemptive history.

4. How long were tongues intended to last? In chapter 6 I will
    answer the crucial question as to whether God intended for
    tongues to get the church started off in the new covenant
    era or were to continue throughout the church's history on
    earth.

Each of these questions is crucial for analyzing and evaluating
the modern phenomenon in terms of its *biblical* warrant.

Scripture encourages us: "do not believe every spirit, but test
the spirits to see whether they are from God (1 John 4:1). And as we
do so, we must analyze every religious movement from a biblical
perspective. The word of God is the final arbiter of all truth, but
especially of religious truth.

As Jesus warns his followers in another context, they must be
careful not to "invalidate the word of God by your tradition" (Mark
7:13). Upon this approach the Lord can promise: "blessed are those
who hear the word of God and observe it" (Luke 11:28).

Therefore, while Jesus was in the Garden of Gethsemane
preparing for his death on the cross, he prays to his Father for his
people: "I have given them Your word. . . . Sanctify them in the
truth; Your word is truth" (John 17:14, 17).

Therefore, regarding tongues specifically, as well as the modern
charismatic revival as a religious movement, we must "examine the

Scriptures . . . to see whether these things are so." With that obligation before us, "come now, and let us reason together" (Isa 1:18).

Chapter 2
THE FORM OF TONGUES:
COMMUNICATION

In studying biblical tongues we must consider their nature in terms of both form and content. In this chapter I will focus on its external form or structure; in the next chapter I will demonstrate its revelational content.

Basically two standard positions are used to explain the biblical form of tongues-speaking: One claims that tongues were ecstatic utterances. These utterances were rhapsodic, incoherent, spiritual ejaculations of prayer and praise with no formal structure or linguistic genealogy discernible. Frequently adherents of this view speak of tongues as a "heavenly language." This view almost universally prevails in charismatic circles today.

The other view holds tongues were a miraculous endowment of the Holy Spirit whereby the charismatically-endowed Christian could speak an historical, foreign human language which he had did not previously use or understand. Thus, tongues were a truly miraculous phenomenon of a remarkable nature.

Tongues Were Structured Languages

That tongues were structured, coherent, foreign languages is evident from the Scriptural record. The following provides incontrovertible evidence in this direction.

1. Argument from first occurrence

The definitive, first-occurrence of tongues was indisputably in the form of structured foreign languages. In Acts 2 the first historical manifestation of tongues-speaking confirms its biblical form:

"And when this sound occurred, the multitude came together, and were bewildered, because they were each one hearing them speak in his own language. And they were amazed and marveled, saying 'Why are not all these who speak Galileans? And how is it that we each hear them in our own language to which we were born. . . . We hear them in our tongues speaking the mighty deeds of God.'" (Acts 2:6–8, 11)

This first occurrence is definitive of biblical tongues, for this is the very experience prophesied by God through the prophet Joel (Joel 2:28–32; Acts 2:16–19) and by the Lord Jesus Christ (Acts 1:5).

2. Argument from later episodes

Subsequent occurrences of tongues-speaking in Acts conform to the pattern established in Acts 2. The very next express reference to tongues is found in Acts 10:45–46. When the Lord opens the hearts of Cornelius and his household to the truth of the gospel of Jesus Christ, they immediately exercise the identical gift:

"And all the circumcised believers who had come with Peter were amazed, because the gift of the Holy Spirit had been poured out upon the Gentiles also. For they were hearing them speaking with tongues and exalting God."

When this event is related to the Jerusalem Church, Peter reports that:

"As I began to speak, the Holy Spirit fell upon them, just as He did upon us at the beginning. . . . If God therefore gave to them the same gift as He gave to us also after believing in the Lord Jesus Christ, who was I that I could stand in God's way?" (Acts 11:15, 17)

Note that Peter carefully defines this experience in terms of the Pentecost event. This is the "same gift"; it falls upon Cornelius's household "just as" does upon Peter and the 120 "at the beginning." Clearly the original Pentecost tongues serve as the paradigm for later manifestations.

3. Argument from identical terminology

All references to tongues-speaking in Scripture employ the same basic terminology, thus indicating identity of form. The Greek word for "tongues" occurring in all instances of tongues-speaking is *glossa*. The Greek word for "speak" in every instance is *laleo*.

Since tongues are not re-defined elsewhere, and since all instances employ the same terminology as in Acts, and since an obvious pattern is set early in Acts, we may safely conclude that the biblical form of tongues was constant. Tongues were foreign, human languages spoken under a miraculous movement of the Holy Spirit.

4. Argument from language analogy

In his Epistle to the Corinthians, Paul defines tongues in terms fully compatible with episodes in Acts. In 1 Corinthians 14:10–11, while in the course of speaking to the Corinthian abuse of tongues, Paul writes:

> "There are, perhaps, a great many kinds of languages in the world, and no kind is without meaning. If then I do not know the meaning of the language, I shall be to the one who speaks a barbarian, and the one who speaks will be a barbarian to me."

Here we must note, first, that Paul *expressly asserts* that no language is *without meaning*. He is comparing tongues to world languages, and he recognizes that all languages have coherent meaning.

But, second, he also observes that at Corinth the gift of tongues is being employed in such a manner that no one *present* could understand the *particular foreign language* spoken. That tongues here are foreign languages is evident in that Paul compares the situation to a meeting between two foreigners.

The Greek word "barbarian" indicates one who speaks a foreign language unknown by the Greek-speaking person. Foreigners do not babble incoherently; they speak structured languages — even though the one to whom they speak might not personally understand the language.

This is precisely the failure of the Corinthian Christians: they are employing their gift of tongues (languages) indiscriminately and, thus, are not benefitting the congregation any more than would a preacher speaking a sermon to them in a foreign language.

5. Argument from biblical principle

Paul enunciates a biblical principle which negates the possibility of tongues being rhapsodic frenzy. In 1 Corinthians 14:32 Paul writes that "the spirits of prophets are subject to prophets." That is, it is not in keeping with the *biblical* concept of spiritual gifts for one to lose control of his psycho-somatic self in an emotional frenzy.

In divine endowments the Lord gifts the whole man — the rational, as well as the emotional aspects of man's being. It is only in paganism that those "gifted of the gods" lose control of themselves as their rationality is overridden by a surging of demonic power.

Consequently, the *form* of tongues in Scripture is that of miraculously granted ability to speak in foreign human languages previously unknown to the speaker.

Before moving on to other matters, though, I will survey several leading texts employed in support of the ecstatic-utterance viewpoint.

Alleged Negative Passages

Three passages are especially important in the pro-charismatic defense. These are all easy to explain in terms of the analysis given above: 1 Corinthians 14:2, 14; 1 Corinthians 13:1; and Romans 8:26.

First Corinthians 14:2

Upon first blush, 1 Corinthians 14 seems to demand non-rational ecstatic utterances. There Paul states that "one who speaks in a tongue does not speak to men, but to God; for no one understands, but in his spirit he speaks mysteries," and "if I pray in a tongue, my spirit prays, but my mind is unfruitful." Nevertheless, these statements are fully compatible with the foreign language interpretation, as we shall see.

Please note the fallacy involved in employing these texts against the human-language position. I will begin by illustrating the matter being dealt with in verse 2. If I were to stand up in my local church and begin speaking Yiddish, no one present would understand me. Not one person in my congregation can read, speak, or understand Yiddish, thus we could say "no one understands" because none could comprehend my speech. Nevertheless, God knows all languages, so I would be speaking to God!

We must realize that Paul is writing to a particular church about their particular situation. As with all epistles, 1 Corinthians is an "occasional letter," that is, a letter dealing with particular historical occasions or issues. When we read, for instance, in 1 Corinthians 5:1, 2 that a public case of fornication is buffeting the church and no one mourns it, we need not conclude that this is a general principle operating in all churches. That is, that all churches have fornicators within them and a membership that does not grieve over the moral defection. Rather, we must understand that this is the situation *at Corinth*. Likewise at Corinth tongues are being used when no one present can understand them. Paul's letter indicates serious problems with pride and division within the church (1 Cor. 1:10; 3:21; 4:7, 18; 5:6; 6:6; 11:18; 12:25; 15:31). Apparently, some are using tongues for prideful reasons rather for corporate ministry.

Furthermore, within the very context of the discussion Paul illustrates the problem by comparing it to a situation in which a foreign language is not understood: "Therefore, if I do not know the meaning of the language, I shall be a foreigner to him who speaks, and he who speaks will be a foreigner to me" (1 Cor. 14:11). Surely we may not surmise that foreign languages are not understandable *at all*; rather they are often not understood in *particular situations*.

We discover an interesting parallel situation in Isaiah 33:19 where God promises future deliverance for Israel from subjugation by a foreign nation: "You will no longer see a fierce people, a people of unintelligible speech which no one comprehends." Surely this does not prove that the nation dominating Israel spoke ecstatically or by means of incoherent babble and that no one in all the world could understand their language! The statement in Isaiah means the common Israelite *present before the conquerors* could not understand their conqueror's language.

Consequently, 1 Corinthians 14:2 is not contrary in the least to the foreign language view of tongues. We must understand this verse in terms of its original audience: it teaches that *at Corinth* those who speak in tongues are not speaking to anyone *present* — because no one present knows the language spoken.

First Corinthians 14:14

In like manner we may adequately explain verse 14, which reads: "For if I pray in a tongue, my spirit prays, but my understanding is unfruitful." Given all the previous support of the foreign language view of tongues, we may interpretively and contextually paraphrase this verse: "If I pray in a tongue, my spirit-gift prays, but my understanding of the truths being spoken bears no fruit in others untrained in the language spoken."

In fact, several modern versions lean in this direction. The Beck translation of the Bible reads: "If I pray in a strange language, my spirit prays, but my mind isn't helping anyone." The Amplified Bible reads: "For if I pray in an (unknown) tongue, my spirit (by the Holy Spirit within me) prays, but my mind is unproductive—bears no fruit and helps nobody."

Paul's statement "my spirit" refers to his spirit-gift. When he says "my mind is unfruitful" he is not saying his rational understanding lay dormant as his emotions swelled within. Rather, he means that his understanding of divine truths known by means of his spiritual endowment produce no fruit in those who hear him when he speaks in a language unknown to them.

The overriding point of Paul's instruction in this context urges gifts be used *for the benefit of others* (cf. vv. 3–6, 12, 19). But if the Corinthians use tongues improperly — when no one knows the language — then they do not edify others in the church.

Interestingly, the word "fruitless" is used elsewhere in the sense of non-production of benefit for others. Note the following examples:

Titus 3:14: "And let our people also learn to maintain good works, to meet urgent needs, that they may not be *unfruitful*." Meeting the "urgent needs" of others is "fruitful" by implication here.

Second Peter 1:8: "For if these things are yours and abound, you will be neither barren nor *unfruitful* in the knowledge of our Lord Jesus Christ." The "fruit" sought is in others (at least in part), as indicated in the preceding verses where Peter lists various other-oriented virtues: self-control, brotherly kindness, love.

Matthew 13:22: "Now he who received seed among the thorns is he who hears the word, and the cares of this world and the deceitfulness of riches choke the word, and he becomes *unfruitful*." The context deals with bearing seed, promoting the gospel among others, and so forth. Again, unfruitfulness is other-oriented.

First Corinthians 14:16 and 17 confirm this interpretation:
> "Otherwise, if you bless with the spirit, how will he who occupies the place of the uninformed say 'Amen' at your giving of thanks, since he does not understand what you say? For you indeed give thanks well, but the other is not edified."

The people who hear such tongues in those contexts cannot declare "amen" — they receive no beneficial impartation of knowledge. How could they say "amen" to something they do not understand? Thus, the exercise of the spiritual gift of tongues *in such circumstances* bears no fruit — it is "unfruitful."

First Corinthians 13:1

Another passage often brought to bear on this discussion is 1 Corinthians 13:1: "Though I speak with the tongues of men and of angels, but have not love, I have become as sounding brass or a clanging cymbal." Here those who hold tongues are ecstatic utterances argue that "tongues of angels" are set in opposition to "men's tongues," indicating a radical difference between them.

The linguistic structure of the phrase militates against the interpretation urged. The two genitival phrase "of men" and "of angels" are both controlled by the one noun "tongues." The two types of tongues, then, are related; they are of a kind. The apparent governing relation between them seems to be that both "tongues" are tools of rational communication, either between men or between angels. They are both structured, coherent language systems.

Furthermore, a question arises in this context: On what basis are we justified in assuming angels communicate ecstatically? Surely they converse and commune in a rational way similar to men. As a matter of fact, everywhere we see angels speaking in Scripture they communicate coherently and rationally. The ecstatic utterance view of this verse is quite contrived.

Romans 8:26

A final passage we will consider as contra-indicative of our position is Paul's statement in Romans 8:26:

> "Likewise the Spirit also helps in our weaknesses. For we do not know what we should pray for as we ought, but the Spirit Himself makes intercession for us with groanings which cannot be uttered."

Charismatics often take the "groanings" here as referring to ecstatic utterances in a special prayer language generated by the Holy Spirit.

This is verse is clearly misconstrued in the charismatic argument. The Greek word behind the translation "cannot be uttered" is *alaletois*. It is a compound of the negative *a* ("no") and *laletois,* "to speak." Thus, literally the groanings are "unspeakable," "unutterable." Whatever this verse refers to, it cannot refer to anything uttered, e.g., tongues-*speaking*!

Chapter 3
THE CONTENT OF TONGUES:
REVELATION

Probably the most misunderstood aspect of the nature of tongues — and in the nature of the case the most dangerous — is the nature of tongues relative to their *content*. Scripture is abundantly clear: *Tongues-speaking is a revelation-bearing gift*. Tongues serve as a mode of direct revelation from God to man. They brought revelation from God to man just as surely as the gift of prophecy brought revelation to the prophets and apostles of old.

Thus, tongues bring inspired, inerrant, absolutely authoritative communication from God to man via the Holy Spirit. Consider the following lines of evidence.

Argument from Initial Occurrence

In Acts 2 tongues are defined as prophetic. When Peter stands up to interpret the Pentecost phenomenon of tongues-speaking causing the amazement of the crowds (Acts 2:6, 12), he categorically states that the episode is *prophetic*:

> "But this is what was spoken by the prophet Joel: 'And it shall come to pass in the last days, says God, That I will pour out of My Spirit on all flesh; your sons and your daughters shall *prophesy*, your young men shall see visions, your old men shall dream dreams, and on My menservants and on My maidservants I will pour out My Spirit in those days; and they shall *prophesy*.'" (Acts 2:16–18)

The biblical concept of godly prophesying is a *speaking forth of the mind and will of God under the direct impulse of the Spirit*. the matter of prophetic claims is so significant that God's Law mandates capital punishment for false prophecy (Deut. 18:20). The claim to speak under the direct impulse and authority of God is a very serious matter.

Argument from Word-gift Relationship

In Scripture tongues are frequently tied up with and related to other revelational gifts (Acts 2; 19; 1 Cor. 13; 14). In the preceding comments above I showed that tongues are related to "prophecy" in Acts 2. The same is true in Acts 19 where we read that the converts both speak with tongues and *prophesy*: "And when Paul had laid hands on them, the Holy Spirit came upon them, and they spoke with tongues and prophesied" (Acts 19:6).

For our present purposes, let us note that 1 Corinthians 13:8 unites tongues with the revelatory spiritual gifts of "knowledge" and "prophecy": "Love never fails. But whether there are prophecies, they will fail; whether there are tongues, they will cease; whether there is knowledge, it will vanish away." In 1 Corinthians 14 Paul considers tongues at great length in conjunction with prophecy. (For information on the "gift of knowledge," see Chapter 5 below.)

A difference between tongues and prophecy exists, to be sure. But they differ in formal structure, rather than content. Prophecy involves the Spirit-endowed ability to speak infallibly the will of God in one's native language. Whereas, the gift of tongues enables the speaker to infallibly declare the will of God miraculously in a language one had never learned.

Argument from Mystery Character

First Corinthians 14:2 states: "For he who speaks in a tongue does not speak to men but to God, for no one understands him; however, in the spirit he speaks mysteries."

Most good Bible dictionaries define the concept of "mystery" in Scripture in terms of revelation from God. For instance, the *Zondervan Pictorial Bible Dictionary* reads: "A mystery (spoken) is thus now a revelation." The Arndt-Gingrich-Danker *Greek-English Lexicon* of New Testament Greek notes that:

> "Our literature uses it [i.e., mystery] to mean the secret thoughts, plans, and dispensations of God, which are hidden from the human reason, as well as from all other comprehension below the divine level, and hence must be revealed to those for whom they are intended."

Bible versions clearly exhibiting this understanding of the term include: Moffatt, Amplified, Williams, Weymouth, Phillips, and Today's English Version.

Conclusion

The nature of *biblical* tongues in terms of their form and content is precisely defined in Scripture itself. The gift of tongues in Scripture is a miraculous endowment of the Holy Spirit of God whereby the gifted are enabled to speak in a foreign language never previously known. It is not a gift of ecstatic, emotionally frenzied, incoherent rhapsody.

The content of tongues is that of a revelatory message given by a direct impulse of the Spirit, the Revealer of Truth. Consequently, the message related in tongues is on par with Scriptural revelation, possessing infallibility, inerrancy, and authority. The modern phenomenon bears no relation to biblical tongues. The modern charismatic experience, therefore, is alien to Scriptures, and is devoid of biblical warrant.

Chapter 4
THE PURPOSE OF TONGUES:
CONFIRMATION

In the study of biblical phenomena it is imperative that we seek out the underlying, compelling divine purposes motivating them. God is a God of order and design: "For God is not the author of confusion but of peace, as in all the churches of the saints" (1 Cor. 14:33). He operates according to his own rational decree, so that when he acts, he acts in terms of a wise plan and a holy goal.

For instance, in Jesus's choice of parabolic discourse as a teaching tool we can discern a biblically-defined purpose. The Lord does not speak in parable to be clever, to appear profound, or to draw crowds. Rather, he expressly informs us that the intent of his parables is to obscure the truth to the non-elect, while opening it up to the elect:

> "And He said to them, 'To you it has been given to know the mystery of the kingdom of God; but to those who are outside, all things come in parables, so that "Seeing they may see and not perceive, and hearing they may hear and not understand; lest they should turn and their sins be forgiven them"'" (Mark 4:11–12).

By the same token miracles in Holy Writ are for a particular purpose. They serve as signs from God, validating the message which they accompany, as in the case of Christ's miracles:

> "And truly Jesus did many other signs in the presence of His disciples, which are not written in this book; but these are written that you may believe that Jesus is the Christ, the Son of God, and that believing you may have life in His name." (John 20:30-31)

In like manner tongues serve a particular divine purpose in the plan of redemption. That purpose is two-fold: (1) Tongues are a validational sign of the apostolic message serving (2) as a sign of covenant curse upon Israel for rejecting that message. In this chapter I will focus on tongues as a sign of apostolic confirmation.

Miraculous phenomena are always attached to revelation from God. In biblical history, eras of new special revelation are punctuated by validating sign-miracles.

Miracles as Validation in the Old Covenant

In Exodus God clearly endows Moses with miraculous power in order to underscore the divine origin of his message. When Moses initially balks at his task, he expresses a concern that the people might say: "The Lord hath not appeared to you" (Exo. 4:1).
In response to this fear the Lord endued him with miraculous abilities (such as the power to turn his staff into a serpent, Exo. 4:3) "that they may believe that the Lord, the God of their father. . . has appeared to you" (Exo. 4:5; cp. Acts 7:36–38).

In 1 Kings when Elijah raises the widow's son from death, the widow exclaims: "Now I know that you are a man of God, and that the word of the Lord in your mouth is truth" (1 Kings 17:24).

In Elisha's ministry at the cleansing of Naaman from leprosy, Naaman says: "Behold, now I know that there is no God in all the earth, but in Israel" (2 Kings 5:15).

The Lord Jesus Christ performs many miracles for this purpose: "Jesus answered them, 'I told you, and you do not believe; the works that I do in My Father's name, these bear witness of Me'" (John 10:25; cf. John 20:30–31).

Miracles as Validation in the New Covenant

As redemptive history progresses into the post-Pentecost, new covenant era we discover the same purpose in the miracles of the revelation-bearing apostles. The Lord confirms their message with many signs and wonders: "Then fear came upon every soul, and many wonders and signs were done through the apostles" (Acts 2:43). "What shall we do to these men? For, indeed, that a notable miracle has been done through them is evident to all who dwell in Jerusalem, and we cannot deny it" (Acts 4:16).

As a matter of fact, Paul, being the late-comer to the apostolate (I Cor. 15:8–9), draws attention to his miraculous signs as proof of his apostleship: "The signs of a true apostle were performed among you with all perseverance, by signs and wonders and miracles" (2 Cor.12:12, cf. also Gal. 3:5; Rom. 15:17–19).

The ability to bestow miraculous gifts upon believers is itself a validational ministry of the apostles. We see this from the following texts.

In Mark 16:17 the Lord promises his disciples that "these signs will accompany those who have believed: in My name they will cast out demons, they will speak with new tongues." This assures the apostles of their authority from God.

After Pentecost, tongues-speaking episodes occur in connection with the apostolic ministry: In Acts 10 after Peter preaches to Cornelius' household, the gift of tongues is poured out upon the converts in the presence of the apostle Peter (Acts 10:44–46). This is important because of Peter's reluctance to minister to the Gentiles (Acts 10:9–16) and the Jerusalem church's alarm (Acts 11:1–3).

In Acts 19 after Paul preaches to the disciples of John the Baptist and lays hands on them, they speak in tongues and prophesy (Acts 19:6).

The Corinthian church is obviously filled with tongues-speakers (cf. 1 Cor. 14: 26–27). This seems related in part to Paul's eighteen month ministry among them, which provides him ample time to endow many of them with charismatic gifts (Acts 18:1, 11).

Paul longs to visit churches and individuals in order to impart spiritual gifts to them. In Romans 1:11 he writes: "For I long to see you in order that I may impart some spiritual gift to you, that you may be established." In 2 Timothy 1:6 Paul writes: "And for this reason I remind you to kindle afresh the gift of God, which is in you through the laying an of my hands."

Consequently, the bestowing of supernatural-miraculous gifts upon believers serves as a confirmation of the apostolic message. This is clearly taught in the *locus classicus* on the matter: "How shall we escape if we neglect so great a salvation? After it was at the first spoken through the Lord, it was confirmed to us by those who heard, God also bearing witness with them, by signs and wonders and by various miracles and gifts of the Holy Spirit according to His own will" (Heb. 2:3, 4).

This is further emphasized in the narrative of the expansion of the apostolic church in Acts: "Therefore they spent a long time there speaking boldly with reliance upon the Lord, who was bearing witness to the word of His grace, granting that signs and wonders be done by their hands" (Acts 14:3).

But now, what about tongues as a sign of covenant curse? I will focus on this topic in the next chapter.

Chapter 5
THE PURPOSE OF TONGUES:
ADMONITION

Probably the least understood aspect of the function of tongues is its serving as a sign to Israel of God's covenant curse due to her unbelief. Yet Paul explicitly suggests this in 1 Corinthians 14:21–22:

"In the Law it is written: 'By men of strange tongues and by the lips of strangers I will speak to this people, and even so they will not listen to Me,' says the Lord. So then tongues are for a sign, not to those who believe, but to unbelievers."

To properly grasp Paul's biblico-theological intent here, I will survey some of the Old Testament's covenantal background, as well as some of the cultural and historical factors influencing the Corinthian church.

Covenantal Backdrop

The Old Testament teaches that Israel was a special people in the sight of God. The Lord richly blessed Israel in terms of his covenant in numerous respects. He was bound in a special, covenantal love to Israel alone of all the nations (Deut. 7:6–8; Amos 3:2). Thus only they received His gracious Law (Deut. 4:10–13; Psa. 147:19, 20), His oracles (Rom. 3:2), the covenantal sign of circumcision (Rom. 3:1) — indeed, all the gracious promises and means of covenant life (Rom. 9:4,5; Eph. 2:12).

The covenant, however, is a two-edged sword. Covenant life was one of both privilege and responsibility. Whereas covenant obedience brought spiritual and material blessings to the people, covenant disobedience brought spiritual and material curses (Deut. 28:15–68). Israel knew full well the two-fold direction of the covenant:

"Now it shall come to pass, if you diligently obey the voice of the
LORD your God, to observe carefully all His commandments which
I command you today, that the LORD your God will set you high
above all nations of the earth . . . . But it shall come to pass, if you
do not obey the voice of the LORD your God, to observe carefully
all His commandments and His statutes which I command you
today, that all these curses will come upon you and overtake
you." (Deut. 28:1, 15; cp. Deut. 30:15–19; Josh. 1:6–9)

Israel voluntarily consented to the covenant, for we read: "All
words which the LORD has spoken we will do" (Exo. 24:3, cp. v 7)
And God dramatically calls heaven and earth to witness to her
acceptance of the covenant:

"I call heaven and earth to witness against you today, that I have
set before you life and death, the blessing and the curse. So
choose life in order that you may live, you and your descendants."
(Deut. 30:19; cp Deut. 32:1; Isa 1–2)

Regarding tongues let us focus on one particular element of
covenantal life for Israel. A vital aspect of covenant blessing for
Israel is national freedom and political self-rule. The Ten Commandments begin by referring to this important truth: "I am the Lord
your God, who brought you out of the land of Egypt, out of the
house of slavery" (Exo. 20:2; Deut. 5:6). See also in this connection
Deuteronomy 6:10–12, 20–24; 7:1–2.

Thus, one aspect of covenant curse would be the loss of national
freedom and self-rule:

"Because you did not serve the LORD your God with joy and
gladness of heart, for the abundance of everything, therefore you
shall serve your enemies, whom the LORD will send against you,
in hunger, in thirst, in nakedness, and in need of everything; and
He will put a yoke of iron on your neck until He has destroyed
you. The LORD will bring a nation against you from afar, from the
end of the earth, as swift as the eagle flies, a nation whose language you will not understand, a nation of fierce countenance,
which does not respect the elderly nor show favor to the young."
(Deut. 28:47–52)

Covenantal Sign

Israel was a nation of people accustomed to receiving signs within their covenant history:

"We do not see our signs; There is no longer any prophet" (Psa. 74:9)

"Then some of the scribes and Pharisees answered, saying, 'Teacher, we want to see a sign from You.'" (Matt. 12:38)

"You brought Your people Israel out of the land of Egypt with signs and with wonders, and with a strong hand and with an outstretched arm, and with great terror." (Jer. 32:21)

"For Jews request a sign, and Greeks seek after wisdom." (1 Cor. 1:22)

Consequently, they were given warning signs indicating that the particular calamities befalling them were indeed the judgment of God (just as the confusion of tongues at Babel expressed the wrath of God, Gen. 10:7–9). The particularly poignant sign of national curse would be the presence of a people speaking a foreign language overrunning the nation (cp. Psa. 81:5; 114:1; Eze. 3:5).

This sign is mentioned in the great covenant blessing and curse chapter, Deuteronomy 28. Citing Deuteronomy 28:49 again, note that: "The Lord will bring a nation against you from afar, from the end of the earth, as the eagle swoops down, a nation whose language you shall not understand" (v. 49; cp. Lev. 26:17).

Other passages highlight this matter quite clearly:

"'Behold, I am bringing a nation against you from afar, O house of Israel,' declares the Lord, 'It is an enduring nation, it is an ancient nation, a nation whose language, you do not know, nor can you understand what they say.'" (Jer. 5:15)

"Indeed, He will speak to this people through stammering lips and a foreign tongue." (Isa. 28:11)

In speaking of the removal of the curse and the return of covenantal blessing, the sign of curse would be removed, as Isaiah prophesies: "You will no longer see a fierce people, a people of unintelligible speech which no one comprehends, of a stammering tongue which no one understands" (Isa. 33:19).

Covenantal Tongues

Clearly, then, the presence of foreign tongues was a sign of curse upon Israel. And all of this is specifically related to the gift of tongues when Paul applies the sign of covenantal curse (Isa. 28:11) to the explanation of tongues:

> In the law it is written: "With men of other tongues and other lips I will speak to this people; and yet, for all that, they will not hear Me," says the Lord. Therefore tongues are for a sign, not to those who believe but to unbelievers. (1 Cor. 14:21–22a).

That Paul lifts this verse out of a passage dealing with covenantal curse is tremendously significant to the tongues debate. To properly grasp its import, we need to survey Isaiah's context.

In Isaiah 28 the Lord rebukes Israel, noting their priests, prophets, and rulers are corrupt drunkards whose tables are filled with vomit and who are ripe for judgment (vv. 1–8). There is no one who can understand the will of God — they are as infants in understanding (v. 9). God had taught them carefully and diligently, line upon line (v. 10); he had promised them rest and peace (v. 12a), but they would not listen (v. 12). So because of this, the nation will stumble and be broken (Isa. 28:13) because rather than the covenant with God, she prefers a covenant with death and Sheol (vv. 14, 15).

In the very heart of God's rebuke through Isaiah we find the verse Paul alludes to in 1 Corinthians — the verse which gives the sign of curse: "Indeed, He will speak to this people through stammering lips and a foreign tongue" (v. 11). Sinful Israel had transgressed the covenant and had refused simple line-by-line instruction in the will of God.

Consequently, their judgment is: they will no longer be spoken to by simple instruction in their native language, but in a foreign tongue by an invading nation. They would be given the sign of judgment. This, of course, refers proximately to the impending Assyrian invasion of Israel. But Paul applies its principle to the future and climactic judgment upon Israel subsequent to their rejection of Christ.

Covenantal Judgment

As we read the New Testament we quickly discover that Christ, "the Messenger of the Covenant" (Mal. 3:1) and the Ratifier of the New Covenant (Luke 22:20), comes to, lovingly courts, and carefully instructs Israel (Matt. 10:5, 6; 15:24; 23:37). Yet Israel refuses His covenantal overtures (Matt. 21:42–45; 23:37–38; John 1:11; Rom. 9:31–32; 10:3). She utterly stumbles over Christ, the Cornerstone of Zion (Matt. 21:42–45; Acts 4:11; Rom. 9:32–33; 1 Pet. 2:7), whom the Lord had promised to send (Isa. 28:16).

The generation to which Christ ministers was rapidly "filling up the measure of the guilt of their fathers" (Matt. 23:32). Consequently, that generation (Matt. 23:36; 24:34) was to receive the fulness of God's covenantal curse: God would send the Roman armies (Luke 21:20) as "his armies" (Matt. 22:7) to raze the temple (Matt. 24:2) which the Lord had left desolate (Matt. 23:38).

Thus, the sign of judgment (foreign tongues) is given to Israel for a period of forty years between Christ's ascension and the A.D. 70 destruction of Jerusalem. God is turning from Israel to the Gentiles (Matt. 21:43; Rom. 9:24–29; 10:19–21).

For forty years Israel, the favored people of God, the guardians of the oracles of God, are given the sign of covenant curse and impending judgment. The nation which had been redeemed (Exo. 14:13; 20:2) to be a kingdom of priests (Exo. 19:6) now receives the word of their God from others — in a foreign tongue.

Covenantal Unbelief

Tongues have a peculiar relevance to Jewish unbelief in this regard. In Acts 2 God attracts the attention of the Jews by tongues-speaking, after which Peter charges them with slaying the Lord of glory (vv. 22–24). The two-edged sword of curse falls upon these men, with the result that many are cut to the heart (Acts 2:37) and repent, thereby leaving apostate Judaism to become Christians (Acts 2:38–41).

Peter cites and applies Joel's prophecy as indicating the coming judgment:

> But this is what was spoken by the prophet Joel: "And it shall come to pass in the last days, says God, that I will pour out of My Spirit on all flesh; Your sons and your daughters shall prophesy, Your young men shall see visions, Your old men shall dream dreams. And on My menservants and on My maidservants I will pour out My Spirit in those days; And they shall prophesy. I will show wonders in heaven above And signs in the earth beneath: Blood and fire and vapor of smoke. The sun shall be turned into darkness, And the moon into blood, before the coming of the great and awesome day of the LORD." (Acts 2:16–20)

Then he warns the Jews: "Be saved from this perverse generation" (Acts 2:40b).

Tongues serve as a sign relevant largely (though not exclusively) to Jewish unbelief in the Corinthian church, as well. Note the following evidence in this regard.

The Corinthian context

The Corinthian church is born in a context both of strong Jewish opposition and impressive Jewish conversions. Acts 18 records that Paul's eighteen month ministry at Corinth (v. 11) was characterized by heated opposition from Judaism.

While teaching at the Corinthian synagogue the Jews' opposition vigorously oppose the gospel message to the point of blasphemy, causing Paul to call down a curse upon them (Acts 18:6). Resistance is so violent that the Lord appears to Paul in a special vision promising divine protection from harm (vv. 12–13).

The Jewish zealots even pummel Sosthenes, a Christian and former leader of the synagogue, before Gallio's judgment seat (Acts

18:17, cp. 1 Cor. 1:1). Yet despite the opposition, Sosthenes and Crispus, while leaders in the synagogue, believe in the Lord and are converted (Acts 18:8, 17) along with many others (v. 8).

The Jewish desire

The epistle to Corinth itself refers to the Jews and their desire for signs (1 Cor. 1:22). We see this Jewish desire in Jesus' experience with Israel: "Then some of the scribes and Pharisees said to Him, 'Teacher, we want to see a sign from You'" (Matt. 12:38). "The Pharisees and Sadducees came up, and testing Jesus, they asked Him to show them a sign from heaven" (Matt. 16:1).

Given the Corinthian church's history this reference to the Jewish concern for signs deserves special significance in regard to the tongues issue. After all this phenomenon receives such prominence in the epistle (three full chapters, 1 Cor. 12–14).

The apostle's warning

Paul's citation of Isaiah 28:11 is lifted out of a passage dealing with covenantal curse upon Israel:

> "In the law it is written: 'With men of other tongues and other lips I will speak to this people; and yet, for all that, they will not hear Me,' says the Lord. Therefore tongues are for a sign, not to those who believe but to unbelievers." (1 Cor. 14:21–22a)

The apostle's is not loosely employing the verse irrespective of its true, contextual meaning. He applies the verse to the tongues issue fully in keeping with its biblico-theological setting. This is tremendously important for the Corinthian church to comprehend. For in chapter ten Paul deals at length with "our fathers" (1 Cor. 14:1) and their disobedience and judgment in the wilderness — and warns the Corinthians of the same predicament if they are not careful (1 Cor. 10:1–12).

Conclusion

In conclusion, tongues truly are "for a sign" (1 Cor. 14:22). The sign had a two-fold, yet inter-related, import: apostolic confirmation and Judaic condemnation. Tongues-speaking is a sign-gift for validating the apostles in their bringing new revelation from God.

The revelational message is, in part, that the final corner had been turned in redemptive history. Whereas, in the past God had dealt almost exclusively with the Jew, he is now-turning from Jewish exclusivism to all men (cp. Acts 1:8; 2:17, 21). The final phase of redemptive history has come, the "last days" has been entered (Acts 2:17; Heb. 1:1; 9:26; 1 Cor. 10:11). The Jews, who reject Christ, are about to fall under the curse of the covenant. This breaks forth in full fury in A.D. 70.

Chapter 6
THE CESSATION OF TONGUES:
COMPLETION

We must approach the question of the transience of tongues — their temporary function and ultimate cessation — biblically and theologically, rather than experientially. In the end we will not resolve the issue of the transience of tongues on the basis of one man's experience — or of a million men's experiences (experience does not establish truth.

Jesus warns about depending on experience in Matthew 7:21–23.:

> "Not everyone who says to Me, 'Lord, Lord,' will enter the kingdom of heaven, but he who does the will of My Father who is in heaven will enter. Many will say to Me on that day, 'Lord, Lord, did we not prophesy in Your name, and in Your name cast out demons, and in Your name perform many miracles?' And then I will declare to them, 'I never knew you; depart from me, you who practice lawlessness.'"

We can resolve the question only upon a "thus saith the Lord" (John 8:31–32; 17:17; Isa. 8:20). With Paul such issues ultimately boil down to this: "Let God be true, but every man a liar" (Rom. 3:4).

According to Scripture, tongues were designed to be a temporary gift to the apostolic church. And thus they have long since faded away from the church. We can see this from at least two clear angles: (1) Their functional purpose has been fully realized, and (2) their biblical end point has been reached.

Tongues' Functional Purpose Realized

As noted above, the functional purpose of tongues is twofold: They served as a sign of validation for the apostolic message and as a sign of covenantal curse upon unbelieving Israel.

Concerning the validation of the apostolic ministry-message, we may draw a helpful illustration from NASA's Space Shuttle program. The launch of the Shuttle was an awe-inspiring technological accomplishment. When in operation the Shuttle perched atop a tremendously powerful booster rocket system which lofted it into orbit.

But not more than a few minutes after a majestic blast-off, after the system has reached an appropriate altitude and speed, the booster rockets fell free from the Shuttle and plunged into the ocean. Why? Why is so much technology and expense poured into the booster rockets only to have them last but a fraction of the voyage —a little more than one minute? The answer is: The booster system *by design* is intended only to get the Shuttle into orbit. If they did not fall away, the entire project would be disastrously jeopardized. The boosters were designed as a temporary mechanism for the space venture.

Likewise tongues served a functional purpose by divine design: In a sense tongues were a part of the "booster stage" of Christianity. Tongues, as a miraculous sign-gift, served to "blast off" the New Covenant era. But once Christianity was safely "on course," tongues (and other miraculous, public sign gifts) were no longer necessary. This analogy illustrating the temporary function of tongues is appropriate, in light of the following observations.

Tongues validated the apostles

Since tongues were a validational sign of the apostles in their revelation-bearing function, once the apostles pass from the historical scene their confirmatory signs would be rendered inoperative. By divine design the apostleship was, in fact, a temporary office, as we see from Scripture:

1. The prerequisite for apostolic office can no longer be met. In Acts 1:22 as the apostles are choosing a successor to fill Judas's vacancy, a particular requirement for the office is stated: "one must be a witness of His resurrection." One who has not seen the Resurrected Lord is excluded from consideration for the apostolate.

Interestingly, Paul defends his own apostleship on this very basis in 1 Corinthians 9:1: "Am I not an apostle? . . . Have not I seen Christ the Lord?" The Lord specifically appeared to Paul to ordain him to the apostolate (Acts 9:1–19; cf. Acts 22:13–15; 26:15–20).

2. Paul specifically informs us that he is the last apostle. "Then He appeared to James, then to all the apostles; and last of all, as it were to one untimely born, He appeared to me also" (1 Cor. 15:7–8). No apostles succeed Paul in history.

3. The apostolic office is a foundational office. It is foundational to the New Covenant phase of the Church. Ephesians 2:19–20 says: "So then you are no longer strangers and aliens, but you are fellow-citizens with the saints, and are of God's household, having been built upon the foundation of the apostles and the prophets, Christ Jesus Himself being the cornerstone." A building's foundation is laid but once, after which the superstructure may be erected for some time.

4. Tongues were gap-fillers. As a revelational gift given to confirm the apostolic message, tongues served to provide supplementary revelation to "fill the gaps" of revelation in the rapidly expanding New Covenant phase of the Church. As the Church expands in geographical outreach she needs a word from God to guide her. The apostles could not be everywhere (1 Cor. 4:17; Rom. 1:11–13; 2 Cor. 8:23), thus revelational gifts (tongues, prophecy, and "knowledge") bring messages from God to supplement the apostolic teaching.

Once the New Testament revelation is finalized, however, such supplementation is no longer needed. The inspired writings of the apostles round out and conclude the canon and can be reproduced and circulated among the churches (cf. e.g., Acts 15:22, 30; 16:4–5; Col. 4:16; Rev. 1:3). Thus, the epistles of the New Testament are often either circular letters to various churches or apostolic responses to specific questions from a church (e.g., Col. 4:16; 1 Thess. 5:27; 1 Cor. 7:1; 12:1).

In anticipation of the closing of the New Testament canon Jude exhorts believers "to earnestly contend for the faith once for all delivered to the saints" (Jude 3). Likewise, Paul can include the soon-to-be-completed body of New Testament writings with the Old Testament books by reference to the complete collection as "Scripture": "All Scripture is inspired of God and profitable" (2 Tim. 3:16).

In fact, Paul cites Luke alongside of Deuteronomy as authoritative: "For the Scripture says, 'You shall not muzzle an ox while it treads out the grain,' and, 'The laborer is worthy of his wages'" (1 Tim. 5:18; cp. Luke 10:7). The continued flow of inspired revelation is not needed after the completion of the New Testament canon. The Bible is a complete, perfectly adequate revelation from God and equips all saints with all they need for every good work (2 Tim. 3:17).

Tongues warned of judgment

Since tongues serve also as a sign of covenant curse upon Israel, once God's curse upon Israel was poured out, such a sign would no longer be necessary.

In this connection, the New Testament teaches that Christ "came to His own, and those who were His own did not receive Him" (John 1:11). That is, for the several years of Christ's ministry, Israel is confronted with the gospel — but refuses it. Consequently, Jesus solemnly warns: "Therefore I say to you, the kingdom of God will be taken away from you, and be given to a nation producing the fruit of it" (Matt. 21:43).

Just a few days later the Lord weeps over Jerusalem in antici-pation of the soon-coming desolation of her temple: "O Jerusalem, Jerusalem, who kills the prophets and stones those who are sent to her! How often I wanted to gather your children together, the way a hen gathers her chicks under her wings, and you were unwilling. Behold, your house is being left to you desolate!" (Matt. 23:37–38).

Israel is filling up the measure of her guilt to completion (Matt. 23:32; 1 Thess. 2:14–16), the ax having already been laid at the root (Matt. 3:10). Soon her desolation will be completed with the devastation of the temple (Matt. 24:2, 34) and Jerusalem itself by invading Roman armies (Luke 21:20, 24). History records the fulfillment of this destruction of Jerusalem in A.D. 70.

Thus the Jews stumble over Christ to their own judgment (Rom. 9:31–33). God issues a solemn covenant warning of judgment. For forty years after the ascension of Christ tongues serve as a sign of impending divine wrath. Tongues serve their purpose right up until the end of the temple.

Tongues' End Point Reached

Paul makes an important statement in First Corinthians that helps us understand the cessation of revelation and revelatory gifts. First Corinthians 13:8–10 reads:

"Love never fails; but if there are gifts of prophecy, they will be done away; if there are tongues, they will cease; if there is knowledge, it will be done away. For we know in part, and we prophesy in part; but when the perfect comes, the partial will be done away."

This passage, properly understood, points to the providential completion of the New Testament canon as that which renders tongues (and other revelatory gifts) inoperative. Tongues, prophecy, and knowledge are specifically designated as having a joint end-point: each will be rendered inoperative at some future date (1 Cor. 13:8). What affects one gift, will affect all three.

Furthermore we must understand that each of the three gifts he mentioned as temporary is a revelatory gift of the Spirit. Who would dispute the claim that prophecy is a revelational gift? We saw earlier in our study that tongues is revelatory.

The nature of the gift

That "knowledge" is a supernatural, revelatory gift and not merely human rationality, is clear in light of the following:

1. It is specifically designated a "spiritual gift" in its context (1 Cor. 12:28). Mundane human rationality or knowledge is not a spiritual gift for the redeemed; it is a "natural" endowment for humanity.

2. The gift is here bound up closely with tongues and prophecy, which are themselves clearly revelatory. Paul seems to specifically be linking tongues with these revelatory gifts.

3. To view "knowledge" here as human rationality is absurd because the context warns that "knowledge" will one day be done away with (1 Cor. 13:8d). Who would teach that in the eternal state (or whenever) there will be no rationality?

The fragmentation of the gift

Now to the point of the transience of tongues as related in this passage. 1 Corinthians 13:9 speaks of these revelatory gifts as piecemeal — they are, by the very nature of the case, fragmented and incomplete revelations: "We know in part (Gk., *ek merous*), and we prophesy in part (Gk., *ek merous*)."

The idea here is simply that during the period between Pentecost and the completion of the canon, God grants a variety of believers in various churches with these revelatory gifts. But these gifts are sporadic in that they give a revelation here and one there. They do not weave a total, complete New Testament revelatory picture. The various prophetic revelations offer at best partial insight into the will of God for the Church.

But 1 Corinthians 13:10 speaks of something coming which will contrast with the piecemeal, bit-by-bit (Greek: *ek merous*) revelation of that transitional, apostolic age. That which supersedes the partial and renders it inoperative is something designated as "perfect" (Gk., *to teleion*): "But when the perfect comes, the partial will be done away."

It is difficult to miss the antithetic parallel between the "partial" thing and the "perfect" (complete, mature, full) thing. The "partial" speaks of the sporadic revelatory gifts of tongues, prophecy, and knowledge. Consequently, it would seem that the "perfect" — which supplants these — represents the perfect and full New Testament Scripture, in that modes of revelation are being contrasted. The final inscripturated word is not piecemeal — it is perfect (James 1:22–25). Thus, it equips the man of God adequately for all the tasks before him (2 Tim. 3:16–17).

This understanding of the intended parallel between piecemeal revelations and the perfect revelation is supported by the following verses. First Corinthians 13:11 illustrates the matter by analogy from Paul's own physical growth. "When I was a child, I used to speak as a child, think as a child, reason as a child; when I became A man, I did away with childish things."

Here we must notice that in verse 10 the contrast is between that which is partial and that which is perfect. Whereas in verse 11 the contrast is between childhood and adulthood. In verses 8 through 10 those things which demonstrate the partial state are three revelatory gifts, whereas in verse 11 he mentions three means of knowledge in the child.

Surely a purposeful parallel exists between the three-fold reference to each of the two states of partiality and childhood: Tongues are equivalent (in the analogy) to "speak as a child," knowledge to "understand as a child," and prophecy to "reason as a child."

The analogy of the gift

The analogy thus presented is this: When Paul was in his childhood he thought as a child, but when he became a mature man he naturally put away childish thought modes. Similarly, when the church was in her infancy stage, she operated by means of bit-by-bit, piecemeal revelation. But when she grew older, she operated through the finalized Scripture. Thus, tongues are related to the church's means of "knowing" in her infancy stage (cp. 1 Cor. 14:19–20).

In 1 Corinthians 13:12 Paul employs another analogy to illustrate the matter: "For now we see in a mirror dimly, but then face-to-face; now I know in part, but then I shall know fully just as I also have been fully known." Paul here is teaching the Corinthians that "now" (Gk., *arti*), "just now, at this present moment"), before the completion and availability of the New Testament canon, they are limited to sporadic, inspired insight into the authoritative will of God. They simply do not know all that God is going to reveal yet. They are looking in a dim mirror. But when they have before them all the New Testament Scriptures, then they will be able to fully see themselves as God sees them, they will know themselves as they really are.

Thus, 1 Corinthians 13 offers important teaching regarding the transience of tongues: both by express reference and by analogy. Tongues are by design intended to serve the Church only during its inter-testamental period while the new covenant revelation is being organized.

Conclusion

In summary, the argument against the continuation of tongues in the Church today is two-fold:

First, the gift of tongues is given for a specific dual purpose. It serves as a sign of confirmation for the apostolic message and as a sign of covenant curse upon unbelieving Israel for rejecting that message about the Messiah. As this two-fold purpose is realized in the first century, tongues were rendered inoperative.

Second, the gift of tongues is given a specific *terminus ad quem* in the very passage which deals most extensively with tongues-speaking in Scripture. First Corinthians 13 teaches that all partial revelational modes are supplanted by the perfect, final revelation — the completed word of God.

Chapter 7
CONCLUSION

Much more needs to be said regarding the tongues-speaking in Scripture, especially as we seek to understand whether or not the wide-spread phenomenon today has biblical warrant. The three basic issues covered in this book, however, are certainly among the more crucial matters for grasping the import of tongues in redemptive history.

The biblical evidence is clear: Tongues-speaking was a God-ordained, temporally-limited, miraculously-endowed grant to first-century Christians for initiating the new covenant.

The tongues spoken in Scripture were foreign languages miraculously given to its recipients. They came upon the recipients without prior study of the language which they suddenly began speaking. Tongues were not rhapsodic, incoherent ejaculations of spiritual frenzy.

In fact, the gift of tongues functioned as a remarkable means of bringing divine revelation to God's people as the new covenant began to unfold in history. The new covenant replaces the old covenant during the apostolic transition period in redemptive history: "When He said, 'A new covenant,' He has made the first obsolete. But whatever is becoming obsolete and growing old is ready to disappear" (Heb 8:13).

Tongues-speaking was one means (among several) whereby God revealed and established the new covenant as the final phase of redemptive history. The writer of Hebrews states:

"How will we escape if we neglect so great a salvation? After it was at the first spoken through the Lord, it was confirmed to us by those who heard, God also testifying with them, both by signs and wonders and by various miracles and by gifts of the Holy Spirit according to His own will." (Heb. 2:13–14)

Furthermore, the New Testament clearly demonstrates, that tongues served as a warning to the Jews of the judgment to befall them in A.D. 70. The temple and its typological worship forms were coming to a conclusion, and the final approach to God moved along more spiritual and direct lines.

Peter interprets the tongues-experience along these lines. He cites Joel in this regard:

"'It shall be in the last days,' God says, 'that I will pour forth of my spirit on all mankind. . . . The sun will be turned into darkness and the moon into blood, before the great and glorious day of the lord shall come." (Acts 2:17, 20)

Therefore, tongues served an important — though temporary — function in their time. Biblical tongues no longer exist, having completed their divine purpose.

HELPFUL RESOURCES

Chantry, Walter, *Signs of the Apostles* (Edinburgh: Banner of Truth, 1973).

Ferguson, Sinclair B., *The Holy Spirit: Contours of Christian Theology* (Downers Grove, Ill.: IVP Academic, 1997).

Gaffin, Richard B., Jr., *Perspectives on Pentecost* (Phillipsburg, N.J.: P & R, 1993).

Gentry, Kenneth L., Jr., *The Charismatic Gift of Prophecy: A Reformed Response to Wayne Grudem* (Fountain Inn, S.C.: Victorious Hope, 2010).

Grudem, Wayne A., ed., *Are Miraculous Gifts for Today?* (Grand Rapids: Zondervan, 1996).

MacArthur, John F., *Charismatic Chaos* (Grand Rapids: Zondervan, 1993).

Robertson, O. Palmer, *The Final Word: A Biblical Response to the Case for Tongues and Prophecy Today* (Edinburgh: Banner of Truth, 1993).

Warfield, Benjamin B., *Counterfeit Miracles* (Edinburgh: Banner of Truth, 1972).